HAL•LEONARD

pro vocal®
BETTER THAN KARAOKE!

SONGBOOK & SOUND-ALIKE CD
WITH UNIQUE PITCH-CHANGER™

VOLUME 33

Billie Holiday

CONTENTS

Cover photo by Photofest

ISBN 978-1-4234-3852-6

HAL•LEONARD®
CORPORATION

7777 W. BLUEMOUND RD. P.O. BOX 13819 MILWAUKEE, WI 53213

Visit Hal Leonard Online at
www.halleonard.com

Crazy He Calls Me

Words by Carl Sigman
Music by Bob Russell

Bridge

do right now.____ The im - pos - si - ble would take a lit - tle

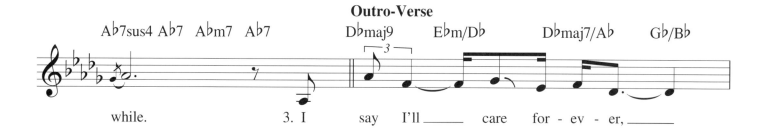

Outro-Verse

while. 3. I say I'll ____ care for - ev - er, ____

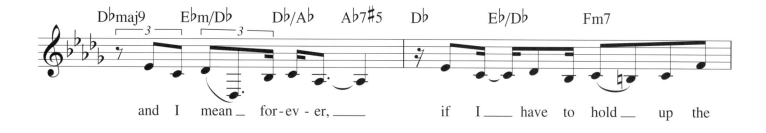

and I mean __ for-ev - er, ____ if I ___ have to hold __ up the

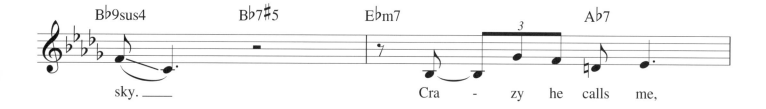

sky. ___ Cra - zy he calls me,

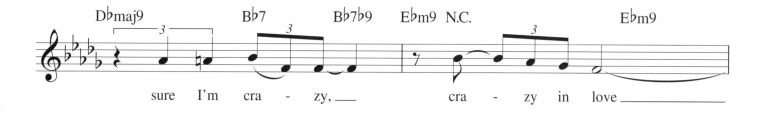

sure I'm cra - zy, __ cra - zy in love _____

Slower

___ am ____ I. ___

Don't Explain

**Words and Music by Billie Holiday
and Arthur Herzog**

Don't Worry 'Bout Me

from COTTON CLUB PARADE

Lyric by Ted Koehler
Music by Rube Bloom

11

God Bless' the Child

from BUBBLING BROWN SUGAR

**Words and Music by Arthur Herzog Jr.
and Billie Holiday**

Easy Living

Theme from the Paramount Picture EASY LIVING

**Words and Music by Leo Robin
and Ralph Rainger**

Peo - ple say you __ rule _____ me with __ one ___ wave __ of your

hand.   Ba - by, it's   grand. _____   They

Outro-Verse

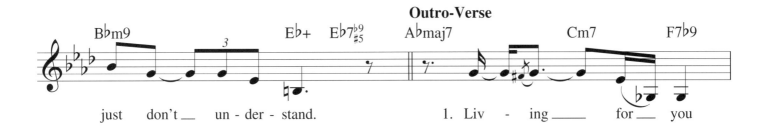

just don't __ un - der - stand.   1. Liv - ing _____ for __ you

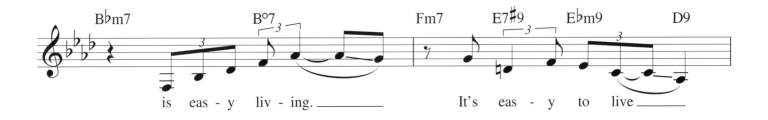

is eas - y liv - ing. _____   It's eas - y to live _____

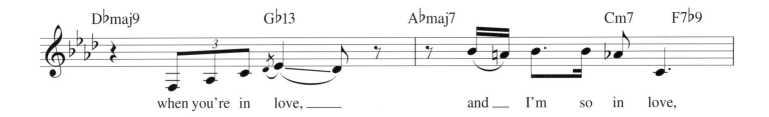

when you're in   love, _____   and __ I'm   so   in   love,

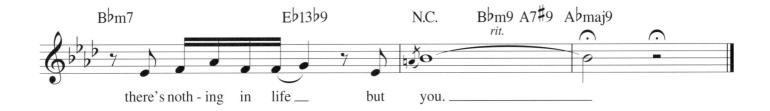

there's noth - ing   in   life __   but   you. _____

Just One More Chance

Words by Sam Coslow
Music by Arthur Johnston

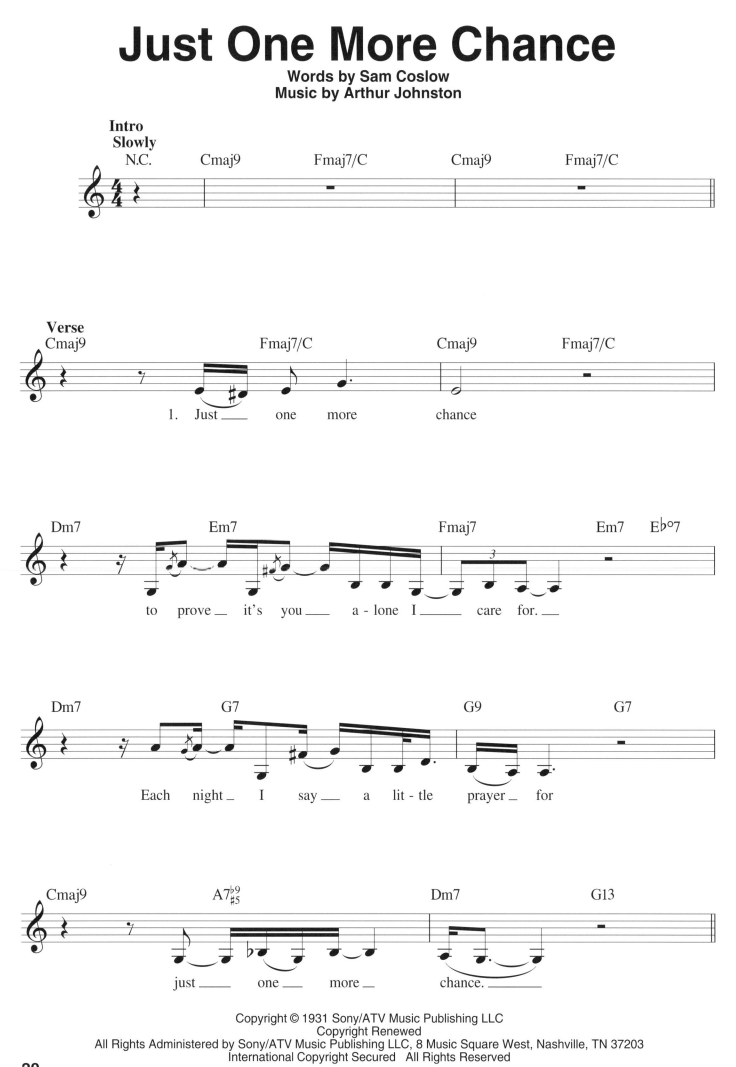

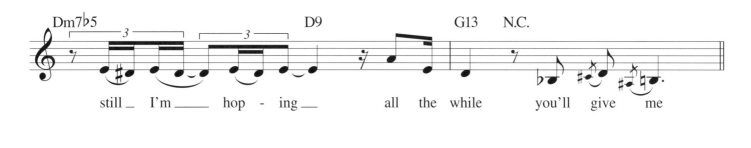

still I'm hop-ing all the while you'll give me

Verse

3. just one more word.

I said that I was glad to start out,

but now I'm back to cry my heart out

for just one more chance.

Interlude-Bridge

I know that I should serve

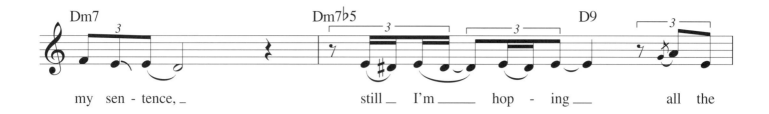

my sen - tence, _ still _ I'm _ hop - ing _ all the

Outro-Verse

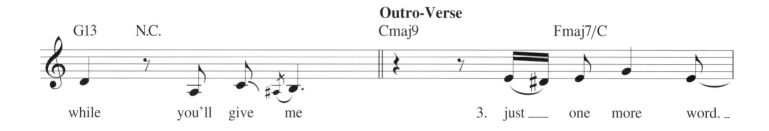

while you'll give me 3. just _ one more word. _

_ I said that I _ was glad _

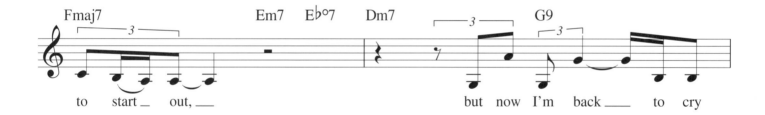

to start _ out, _ but now I'm back _ to cry

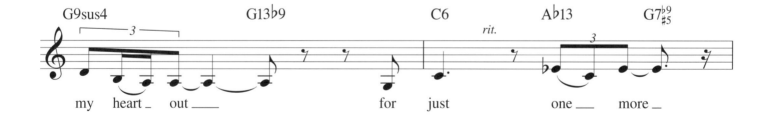

my heart _ out _ for just one _ more _

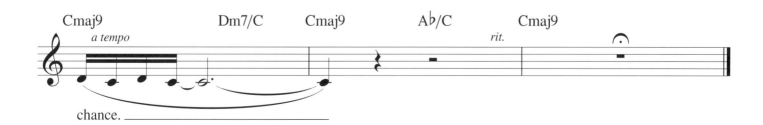

chance. _____

Solitude

**Words and Music by Duke Ellington,
Eddie De Lange and Irving Mills**

Cm7   D♭m6   B♭9   A°7

you   taunt _____   me _____   with _

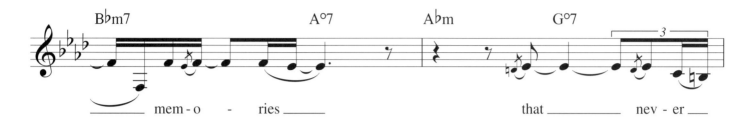

B♭m7   A°7   A♭m   G°7

_____ mem - o - ries _____   that _____ nev - er _

A♭6   E♭m9   D7$^{\sharp 11}_{\sharp 9}$ **Bridge**   D♭maj7   D♭6

die.   I _____   sit   in   my   chair,

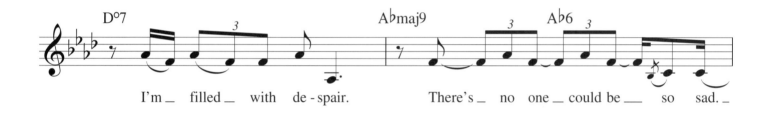

D°7   A♭maj9   A♭6

I _ filled _ with   de - spair.   There's _ no   one _ could be _ so   sad. _

A♭maj9   D♭6

_   With _____   gloom ___   ev - 'ry - where,

D°7   A♭maj7/E♭   Cm7   Bm7

I   sit   and   I   stare.   I _____   know   that   I'll _____   soon   go _

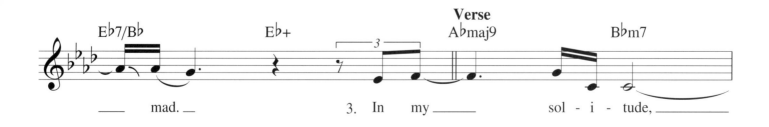

E♭7/B♭   E♭+   **Verse**   A♭maj9   B♭m7

____ mad. _   3. In   my _____   sol - i - tude, _____

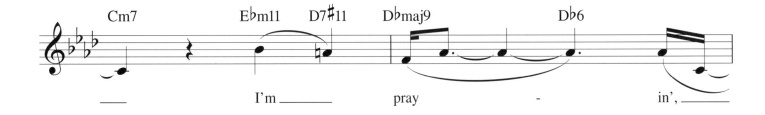

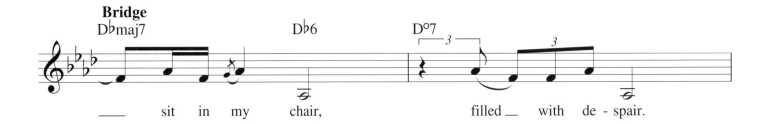

Bridge

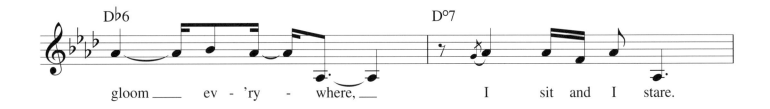

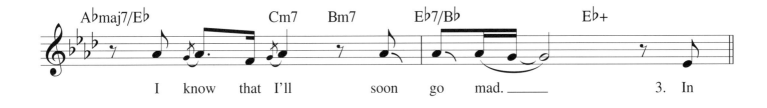

I know that I'll soon go mad. _____ 3. In

Outro-Verse

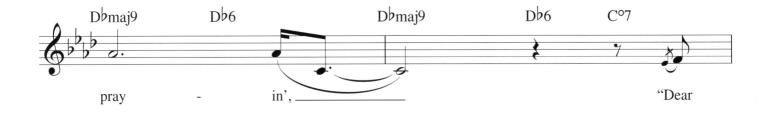

my _____ sol - i - tude, _____ I'm

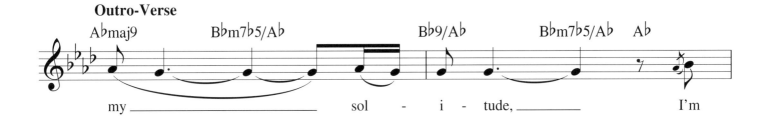

pray - in', _____ "Dear

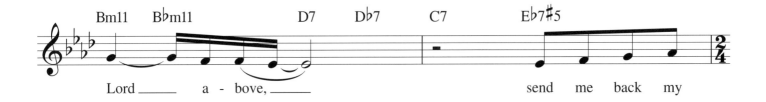

Lord _____ a - bove, _____ send me back my

Bright tempo

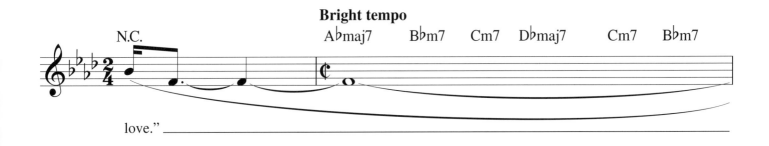

love." _____

Trav'lin' Light

Words by Johnny Mercer
Music by Jimmy Mundy and Trummy Young

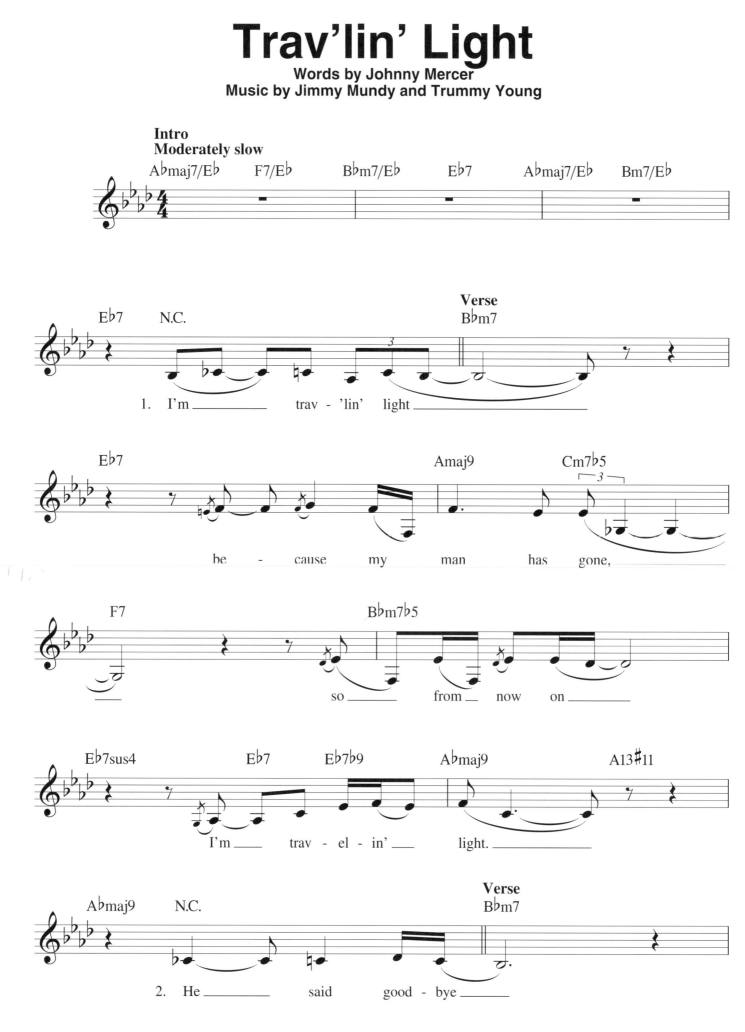

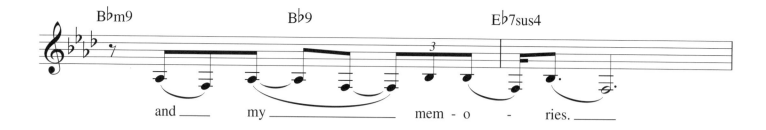

and _____ my _____ mem - o - ries. _____

Outro-Verse

3. Some _____ luck - y _____ night _____

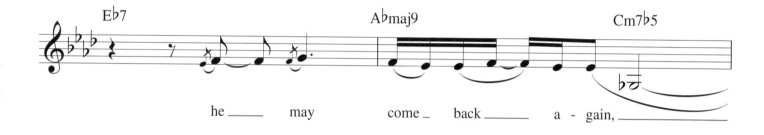

he _____ may come _ back _____ a - gain, _____

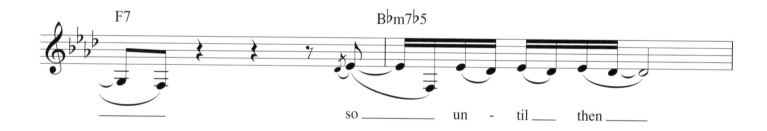

so _____ un - til _____ then _____

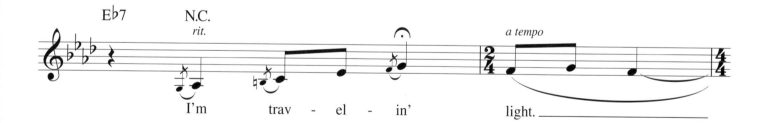

I'm trav - el - in' light. _____

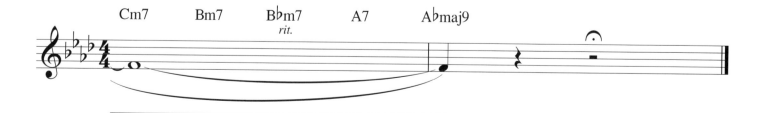

Pro Vocal® Series

SONGBOOK & SOUND-ALIKE CD
SING 8 CHART-TOPPING SONGS WITH A PROFESSIONAL BAND

Whether you're a karaoke singer or an auditioning professional, the Pro Vocal® series is for you! Unlike most karaoke packs, each book in the ProVocal Series contains the lyrics, melody, and chord symbols for eight hit songs. The CD contains demos for listening, and separate backing tracks so you can sing along. The CD is playable on any CD player, but it is also enhanced so PC and Mac computer users can adjust the recording to any pitch without changing the tempo! Perfect for home rehearsal, parties, auditions, corporate events, and gigs without a backup band.

BROADWAY SONGS
00740247 Women's Edition........................$12.95
00740248 Men's Edition............................$12.95

MICHAEL BUBLÉ
00740362 ....$14.95

CHRISTMAS STANDARDS
00740299 Women's Edition........................$12.95
00740298 Men's Edition............................$12.95

KELLY CLARKSON
00740377 ....$14.95

PATSY CLINE
00740374 ....$14.95

CONTEMPORARY HITS
00740246 Women's Edition........................$12.95
00740251 Men's Edition............................$12.95

DISCO FEVER
00740281 Women's Edition........................$12.95
00740282 Men's Edition............................$12.95

DISNEY'S BEST
00740344 Women's Edition........................$14.95
00740345 Men's Edition............................$14.95

DISNEY FAVORITES
00740342 Women's Edition........................$14.95
00740343 Men's Edition $14.95

'80S GOLD
00740277 Women's Edition........................$12.95
00740278 Men's Edition............................$12.95

ELLA FITZGERALD
00740378 ....$14.95

GREASE
00740369 Women's Edition........................$14.95
00740370 Men's Edition............................$14.95

JOSH GROBAN
00740371 ....$17.95

HIGH SCHOOL MUSICAL 1 & 2
00740360 Women's Edition........................$14.95
00740361 Men's Edition............................$14.95

HANNAH MONTANA
00740375 ....$14.95

HIP-HOP HITS
00740368 Men's Edition............................$14.95

HITS OF THE '70S
00740384 Women's Edition........................$14.95
00740383 Men's Edition $14.95

JAZZ BALLADS
00740353 Women's Edition........................$12.95

JAZZ FAVORITES
00740354 Women's Edition........................$12.95

JAZZ STANDARDS
00740249 Women's Edition........................$12.95
00740250 Men's Edition............................$12.95

JAZZ VOCAL STANDARDS
0074037 Women's Edition.........................$14.95

Prices, contents, & availability subject to change without notice.
Disney charaters and artwork © Disney Enterprises, Inc.

FOR MORE INFORMATION, SEE YOUR LOCAL MUSIC DEALER,
OR WRITE TO:

7777 W. BLUEMOUND RD. P.O. BOX 13819 MILWAUKEE, WI 53213

MOVIE SONGS
00740365 Women's Edition........................$14.95
00740366 Men's Edition............................$14.95

MUSICALS OF BOUBLIL & SCHÖNBERG
00740350 Women's Edition........................$14.95
00740351 Men's Edition............................$14.95

ELVIS PRESLEY
00740333 Volume 1....................................$14.95
00740335 Volume 2....................................$14.95

R&B SUPER HITS
00740279 Women's Edition........................$12.95
00740280 Men's Edition............................$12.95

FRANK SINATRA CLASSICS
00740347 ....$14.95

FRANK SINATRA STANDARDS
00740346 ....$14.95

TORCH SONGS
00740363 Women's Edition........................$12.95
00740364 Men's Edition............................$12.95

TOP HITS
00740380 Women's Edition........................$14.95

ANDREW LLOYD WEBBER
00740348 Women's Edition........................$14.95
00740349 Men's Edition............................$14.95

WEDDING GEMS
00740309 Book/CD Pack Women's Edition............$12.95
00740310 Book/CD Pack Men's Edition..................$12.95
00740311 Duets Edition.....................................$12.95

HANK WILLIAMS
00740386 ....$14.95

Visit Hal Leonard online at www.halleonard.com